1/2000

TOP 10 HEISMAN TROPHY WINNERS

Jeff Savage

SPORTS TOP 10

Enslow Publishers, Inc.

44 Fadem Road   PO Box 38
Box 699   Aldershot
Springfield, NJ 07081   Hants GU12 6BP
USA   UK

Library of Congress Cataloging-in-Publication Data

Savage, Jeff.
    Top 10 Heisman trophy winners / Jeff Savage.
        p. cm. — (Sports top 10)
    Includes bibliographical references (p. 46) and index.
    Summary: Highlights the lives and careers of ten winners of the Heisman
trophy: Marcus Allen, Tim Brown, Ernie Davis, Tony Dorsett, Doug Flutie,
Eddie George, Archie Griffin, Paul Hornung, Barry Sanders, and Roger
Staubach.
    ISBN 0-7660-1072-4
    1. Football players—United States—Biography—Juvenile literature.
2. Heisman Trophy—Juvenile literature. 3. Football players—Rating of—
United States—Juvenile literature. 4. College sports—United States—
Juvenile literature. [1. Football players.] I. Title. II. Series.
GV939.A1S254   1999
796.332'092'273—dc21
[B]   98-12023
                                                 CIP
                                               AC

Printed in the United States of America

10 9 8 7 6 5 4 3 2 1

Illustration Credits: Boston College/Mike Sleeper, p. 25; Boston College/
Tim Morse, p. 23; Navy Sports Information Office, pp. 43, 45; Notre Dame
University, p. 37; Notre Dame University/Steven Nauratil, pp. 10, 13; Ohio
State Sports Information, pp. 26, 29, 30, 33; Oklahoma State University
Department of Athletics, pp. 38, 41; Paul Hornung, p. 35; Photo courtesy of
Syracuse University, pp. 14, 17; University of Pittsburgh/Herb Ferguson, pp.
19, 21; University of Southern California Sports Information, pp. 7, 9.

Cover Illustration: University of Southern California Sports Information.

Cover Description: Marcus Allen of the University of Southern California,
1981.

Interior Design: Richard Stalzer.

CONTENTS

INTRODUCTION	4
MARCUS ALLEN	6
TIM BROWN	10
ERNIE DAVIS	14
TONY DORSETT	18
DOUG FLUTIE	22
EDDIE GEORGE	26
ARCHIE GRIFFIN	30
PAUL HORNUNG	34
BARRY SANDERS	38
ROGER STAUBACH	42
CHAPTER NOTES	46
INDEX	48

INTRODUCTION

DOZENS OF COLLEGE FOOTBALL AWARDS are given each year. There is an award for the nation's best quarterback, the best defensive back, the best linebacker, the best Division I-AA player, and the best Division II player. There are even two awards given to the best lineman. It seems that new awards are added every year. With so many trophies being handed out, it is hard to tell who is truly the best.

The Heisman Memorial Trophy is a symbol of greatness. It is awarded each year to the best college football player in the country. The award can be given to a quarterback, a running back, a flanker, or a player at any other position. It can go to a player whose team finished first in the country or to one whose team suffered a losing record. It can go to a senior, a junior, a sophomore, or a freshman. Anyone can win the Heisman. It takes dedication, desire, hustle, and a little luck. Most of all, it takes talent.

Why is the award called the Heisman Memorial Trophy? The bronze statue is named for John W. Heisman, a college coach at the turn of the twentieth century. Heisman is considered by many to be the originator of the center snap, the lateral, and the forward pass. His Georgia Tech team still holds the record for largest margin of victory, defeating Cumberland, 222–0. After coaching, Heisman served as athletic director for a New York City organization known as the Downtown Athletic Club. Its members gathered each weekend to root for their favorite sports teams. In 1935, Heisman's club decided to award a trophy to the best college football player east of the Mississippi River.

But who would choose the player? Heisman figured those who knew sports best were the sportswriters. So when the 1935 season ended, he asked a group of sportswriters to cast their votes. The winner was Jay Berwanger, a running back from the University of Chicago. Berwanger was brought to New York and presented with the Downtown Athletic Club Trophy. A year later, players across the country became eligible for the trophy. Then Heisman died. To honor him, the Downtown Athletic Club renamed its trophy the Heisman Memorial Trophy.

The Heisman winner is still decided today by the nation's sportswriters, along with each of the past winners. The top four or five candidates and their families are invited to the Downtown Athletic Club, where the winner is announced. Until that moment, only the few club members who tallied the votes know who will win.

Choosing the top ten Heisman Trophy winners in history was not easy. Of the ten players we chose, not all became pro football superstars. To us, though, it seemed that each of these ten winners had a Heisman season filled with magic. Here is *our* top ten list.

CAREER STATISTICS

Player	School	Year	Grade	Position
MARCUS ALLEN	USC	1981	SR.	RB
TIM BROWN	Notre Dame	1987	SR.	WR
ERNIE DAVIS	Syracuse	1961	SR.	RB
TONY DORSETT	Pittsburgh	1976	SR.	RB
DOUG FLUTIE	Boston College	1984	SR.	QB
EDDIE GEORGE	Ohio State	1995	SR.	RB
ARCHIE GRIFFIN	Ohio State	1974–75	JR.–SR.	RB
PAUL HORNUNG	Notre Dame	1956	SR.	QB-HB
BARRY SANDERS	Oklahoma State	1988	SR.	RB
ROGER STAUBACH	Navy	1963	JR.	QB

MARCUS ALLEN

ON A HOT SUMMER DAY in southern California in 1981, USC senior tailback Marcus Allen sat down with offensive coordinator John Jackson. The player and coach were about to set some goals for the upcoming season. Allen spoke first. "Hey," he announced, "I want to get 2,000 yards this year."[1]

Coach Jackson gave Allen a curious look. No college player had ever gained 2,000 yards. Such an idea seemed outrageous. "Then," Allen said, "we settled down and made some realistic goals."[2]

Allen opened the season with 210 yards and 4 touchdowns against Tennessee. Then, he reeled off 274 yards against Indiana. Jackson and the other coaches began to wonder. When he gained 208 more against Oklahoma, that outrageous goal suddenly seemed more realistic. Allen ran for 233 yards against Oregon State, then 211 against Arizona, and he was on his way. After a 147-yard performance against mighty Notre Dame, Irish coach Gerry Faust described him as "unbelievable."[3] When he ripped Washington State for 289 yards, Cougars coach Jim Walden called him "Superman."[4]

Finally, on a rain-soaked field at Husky Stadium in Seattle, Allen slogged around right end for 13 yards against Washington to reach the magic number, 2,000. It was fitting that the play was USC's famous power sweep, the "Student Body Right." Allen gained 155 yards that day, then closed his record season the following week at the Los Angeles Coliseum with another 219 yards against rival UCLA. His final run of the season was a 5-yard leap over the Bruins

MARCUS ALLEN

Marcus Allen breaks into the open field for a long gain. In 1981, Allen became the first Division I player to rush for 2,000 yards in a season.

defense to the end zone for a last-second, game-winning touchdown. His yardage total: 2,342.

Marcus Allen was raised by his parents in San Diego. When Marcus was twelve, his father, a carpenter, took him and his brother to work one scorching hot day. Marcus and his brother were sent up a ladder with a hammer and bag of nails to put in shingles. Several hours later, the weary boys finished their work and came down. "Want a regular job?" Marcus's father asked. "No thanks," said Marcus. "We've decided to go to college. There's got to be something better than this."[5]

Allen always kept humble. As he trudged home from practice one day, still wearing his uniform, a car pulled up alongside of him. The driver offered to give him a ride home. Allen recognized the man immediately. It was Mike Garrett, the Heisman Trophy running back from USC. "How good are you?" Garrett asked as they rode off. "Pretty good," Allen admitted. "How good is pretty good?" Garrett asked. Allen didn't want to brag, even to the great Mike Garrett. "I'm okay," he said, shrugging.[6]

Allen was better than that. Playing quarterback in the county championship game his senior year, he scored all five of his team's touchdowns. His team won, 34–6.

He was recruited as a quarterback or tailback by nearly every major college in the country. USC wanted him as a defensive back. He chose USC anyway. "I'd rather play tailback," Allen admitted, "but there's nothing like a USC football Saturday in the world."[7] Soon he was playing his favorite position, setting unrealistic goals, and reaching them.

After USC, Allen played 16 seasons in the NFL, for the Los Angeles Raiders and Kansas City Chiefs. He retired after the 1997 season, having gained 12,243 yards in his career. At the time of his retirement, Allen held the NFL record for most rushing touchdowns with 123.

Marcus Allen

BORN: March 26, 1960, San Diego, California.

HIGH SCHOOL: Lincoln High School, San Diego, California.

COLLEGE: University of Southern California.

PRO: Los Angeles Raiders, 1982–1992; Kansas City Chiefs 1993–1998.

HONORS: Heisman Trophy, 1981; Maxwell Award (outstanding college player), 1981; Super Bowl XVIII MVP; NFL Most Valuable Player, 1985.

Dodging through the Cougars defense, Allen heads for the end zone. Allen was the first college back to run for over 2,000 yards in a season.

TIM BROWN

Tim Brown was a dangerous weapon in the Notre Dame offense, and on special teams. During his career he caught passes, ran the ball, and returned kickoffs and punts.

TIM BROWN WAS THE MOST DANGEROUS player in college football. Everyone knew it. Brown had already set a Notre Dame record for total yardage. His all-purpose average in 1986—for catching passes, returning kicks, and running with the ball—ranked second in the nation. USC coach Ted Tollner knew about Brown. In the season finale at the Los Angeles Coliseum, the fleet junior had already caught passes for 89 yards, rushed for 10 more, and returned kickoffs for another 97. Now, with three minutes left, and USC clinging to a 37–35 lead, Brown was dropping back to return a punt.

Brown had returned only one punt in his college career, but Tollner took no chances. He told his punter to kick the ball to the sideline, away from Brown. The punter did as he was told. But as the ball sailed toward the sideline, Brown raced over and snared it on the fly. He spun away from one defender and skipped past another. He swerved through the Trojans defenders as if they were pylons. He was finally tackled deep in USC territory where, moments later, on the last play of the game, kicker John Carney drilled a 19-yarder to win it.

"I was nervous," Brown admitted later. "I was worried about catching the ball. But once I caught it, the rest came easy. I knew I could run with it."[1]

Brown has been running with a football as long as he can remember. From Pee Wee League through high school he played quarterback, running back, wide receiver, kick returner, and safety. At Woodrow Wilson High School in Dallas, Texas, he returned 6 kickoffs and 3 punts for touchdowns in three seasons. "It really has a lot to do with peripheral vision," Brown said about returning kicks. "If you can't see that guy coming at you from the side, you're going to get nailed."[2]

Brown never liked being the center of attention. Even at his local church, he preferred to play the bass drum from the rear of the ensemble. "I would just get in the back," he said, "and try to help make the rest of the choir sound good."[3]

Brown caught everyone's attention in high school. He was an A student in the classroom, and his teachers and classmates admired him for it. On the football field, he was his team's lone star. Opponents learned that if they stopped him, they would win, so they double- and triple-teamed him on every play. The strategy usually worked. His school recorded a miserable record of 4–25–1 in his three seasons.

Everything stayed the same for Brown at Notre Dame except the losing. He took academics seriously. He kept humble. And when he touched the football, exciting things usually happened. He scored 22 touchdowns for Notre Dame, and the average gain for each touchdown was over 42 yards, or nearly half the football field. He ran back punts and kickoffs for more yards and touchdowns than anyone else in Notre Dame history. "Tim is the most gifted, talented player that I've ever been around," said Irish coach Lou Holtz.[4]

Since Brown's Heisman Trophy senior season in 1987, he's made plenty of NFL coaches feel the same way. He has been an All-Pro receiver for the Oakland Raiders, and holds the NFL record for most punt returns.

TIM BROWN

BORN: July 22, 1966, Dallas, Texas.

HIGH SCHOOL: Woodrow Wilson High School, Dallas, Texas.

COLLEGE: University of Notre Dame.

PRO: Los Angeles/Oakland Raiders, 1988– .

HONORS: Heisman Trophy, 1987; First-team All-America, 1986, 1987; Kodak All-America, 1987.

Running with the ball, Tim Brown scans for defenders. In 1987, Brown was named the College Football Player of the Year by *The Sporting News*.

ERNIE DAVIS

Known as the "Elmira Express," Ernie Davis went to Syracuse University to follow in the footsteps of his idol, Jim Brown.

ERNIE DAVIS

THE AIR WAS FRIGID, the ground was frozen solid, and the Syracuse Orangemen were desperate. They were trailing the University of Miami, 14–0, in the 1961 Liberty Bowl. The Orangemen turned to their star halfback, Ernie Davis. It would not be easy running on the frozen turf, but Davis smiled anyway. Davis always smiled.

As a boy, Davis often played on frosty fields in the Philadelphia area where he grew up. Running in harsh conditions was nothing new to him. And with his family and friends watching from the stands, Davis rammed into the teeth of the Miami defense over and over again. "He carried three or four tacklers on his back every carry," Syracuse coach Ben Schwartzwalder remembered. "Ten guys stood around and watched him."[1] When it was over, Davis had bulldozed for 140 yards and carried his team to a 15–14 victory. It was the perfect ending to a fabulous college career.

Ernie Davis was born in New Salem, Pennsylvania, and lived with his grandmother in nearby Uniontown. His mother was unable to raise him, and he never knew his father. But when life got tough, Davis just tried harder to smile. He remembered being eight years old and walking nearly six miles each day to practice with a Midget League team. But when the time came for uniforms to be passed out, Davis did not get one. "I kept standing around," he said, "trying not to cry."[2]

When Davis turned twelve, he went to live with his mother in Elmira, New York, where he became a sports star at Elmira Free Academy. He led his basketball team to a state record 52 straight victories, and he ran so swiftly with the football that he became known as the Elmira Express. His hero was Syracuse running back Jim Brown, who later starred for the Cleveland Browns. Brown visited Davis one day and encouraged him to go to Syracuse. Davis joined the Orangemen and was issued jersey No. 44, Brown's old number.

As a sophomore, Davis led Syracuse to an undefeated season, and the school's first-ever national championship. As a junior, he averaged 7.8 yards per carry and broke several of Brown's records. As a senior, he single-handedly outscored Syracuse's opponents, broke the rest of Brown's records, and was an easy choice for the Heisman Trophy. He was the first African American to win the award.

Moments after Davis was presented the award, he was whisked away by cab to a nearby hotel, where President John F. Kennedy was waiting. President Kennedy had asked to meet Ernie Davis. "I never thought I'd get the honor of shaking hands with the president," Davis said. "It was a big thrill for me, the biggest next to winning the Heisman award."[3]

The Washington Redskins made Davis the NFL's No. 1 draft pick in 1962, then traded him to the Cleveland Browns for All-Pro Bobby Mitchell. Davis and Jim Brown were going to play in the backfield together for the Browns. Then Davis got sick.

Doctors discovered that Davis had leukemia, a form of blood cancer. There was no known cure at that time. But Davis felt fine, and he was sure he would overcome his illness. He spent much of his time with the Browns. One day he told the other players he had to go into the hospital for some treatment. He entered the hospital, and the following day he went into a coma. Early the next morning he died. "It will be a long time," said Browns owner Art Modell, "before we again see a boy like Ernie Davis as either an athlete or a man."[4]

ERNIE DAVIS

BORN: December 14, 1939, New Salem, Pennsylvania.

DIED: May 18, 1963, Elmira, New York.

HIGH SCHOOL: Elmira Free Academy, Elmira, New York.

COLLEGE: Syracuse University.

PRO: Drafted by Washington Redskins; traded to Cleveland Browns (never played).

HONORS: Heisman Trophy, 1961; College Football Hall of Fame.

After winning the Heisman Trophy, Ernie Davis had the honor of meeting President John F. Kennedy.

TONY DORSETT

TONY DORSETT SAT IN THE PITTSBURGH locker room at halftime with a worried look on his face. His Pitt Panthers weren't losing, but they weren't winning either. They were locked in a 7–7 tie with mighty Penn State. Dorsett's team needed to win this game to finish the 1976 season undefeated. But the Panthers hadn't beaten their rival in eleven years. It wouldn't be easy.

Dorsett had averaged 215 yards rushing in his last six games, and Penn State coach Joe Paterno knew his team had to stop the great tailback to win. Paterno used sixteen different alignments in the first half to try to confuse Dorsett. The strategy worked. Dorsett managed only 51 yards in the half.

Pitt coach Johnny Majors countered with a trick of his own. He switched Dorsett to fullback. The trick worked. In play after play, Dorsett burst through the line before the Nittany Lions could react. When it was over, Dorsett had rushed for 224 yards and 2 touchdowns. Pitt won, 24–7. "I didn't think they could run up the gut like that on us," said Paterno. Asked to describe Dorsett, the coach said, "How many ways can you say great?"[1]

Tony Dorsett grew up in the shadows of the steel mills of Pittsburgh, Pennsylvania. He lived with his parents in a dangerous area of Aliquippa, where gangs roamed the streets. When gang fights started, Dorsett would turn and run. "I was too scared to fight those big guys," he said. "That's how I think I got so fast—running away from those bloody fights."[2]

Dorsett's mother called him Turtle because he moved so slowly. His father called him Hawk for his big brown eyes.

Tony Dorsett charges through the line, and gains some tough yards.

TONY DORSETT

By the time he was in high school, everyone was calling him T.D. for his initials, and for what he did on the football field. He averaged two touchdowns a game his senior year, and one magazine proclaimed him the best prep player in the country. He was recruited heavily by USC, which was famous for its running backs, but he was afraid to move to California. He chose the University of Pittsburgh. "He was a very shy, introverted kid when he came here," said Pitt sports information director Dean Billick. "He wasn't ready for what hit him."[3]

No one was. Dorsett ran for 101 yards against Georgia in his first college football game, 265 yards against Northwestern in his third game, then 211 against Syracuse and 209 against Notre Dame. Panthers backfield coach Harry Jones said, "T.D. is quicker than a hiccup and tougher than week-old bread."[4]

By the time T.D.'s college career ended, he had set eleven NCAA records, tied three others, and set twenty-eight school records. He became the first collegian ever to run for at least 1,000 yards all four seasons, and the first to gain more than 6,000 total. He was a runaway choice for the 1976 Heisman Trophy before moving on to the NFL and a Hall of Fame career with the Dallas Cowboys. "Every record I've set [my family] has seen," Dorsett said. "That's the sweetest thing about it. My parents are proud of me, my brothers are proud of me, and my friends are proud of me. That's a nice feeling."[5]

TONY DORSETT

BORN: April 7, 1954, Aliquippa, Pennsylvania.

HIGH SCHOOL: Hopewell High, Aliquippa, Pennsylvania.

COLLEGE: University of Pittsburgh.

PRO: Dallas Cowboys, 1977–1987; Denver Broncos, 1988.

HONORS: Heisman Trophy, 1976; Maxwell Award (outstanding college player), 1976; NFL Rookie of the Year, 1977; NFL Player of the Year, 1981; College Football Hall of Fame; Pro Football Hall of Fame, 1994.

Breaking away from the defense, Tony Dorsett looks for another hole. Dorsett was the first player to rush for 1,000 yards in each of his four college seasons.

DOUG FLUTIE

THE RAIN WAS BLOWING SIDEWAYS. It was the day after Thanksgiving, 1984, and the Boston College Eagles were fifteen hundred miles from home. They trailed by four points. The ball was at the 48-yard line. The clock was down to six seconds. The defending national champion Miami Hurricanes were on defense. Boston College coach Jack Bicknell was on the sideline, "thinking about what I'm going to say to the kids after the loss."[1]

Doug Flutie was in the Boston College huddle. "Fifty-five flood tip," Flutie said to his teammates. The Eagles broke the huddle, and three receivers lined up to the right. Among them was Gerard Phelan, Flutie's roommate and best friend. The ball was snapped, and Flutie dropped back to pass. He scrambled to his right, stopped, and looked downfield. He planted his feet, reared back, and threw into the gusting wind and rain. The ball spiraled sixty-five yards in the air. A national television audience saw it sail over the head of three Miami defenders . . . and into the arms of Phelan.

Anyone who saw it will never forget it. There was Phelan, jumping up from the muddy turf to show the referee he had the ball. There were the Miami players, collapsing to the ground in disbelief. And there was Flutie, racing downfield with flailing arms to hug his best friend. In one of the most thrilling plays in football history, Boston College had shocked Miami, 47–45.

Doug Flutie was born in Manchester, Maryland, and his family moved to Melbourne, Florida, when he was five. He grew up with a love for sports. "If it was a rainy day and we

DOUG FLUTIE

Doug Flutie drops back to unload a bomb. Because of his lack of height, many thought that Flutie would not be able to succeed as a quarterback.

couldn't play outdoors, Doug would make up games we could play in the basement," his brother Bill remembers. "He'd crush a paper cup and make believe it was a ball. We'd play what he called Paper Cup Baseball downstairs. Our hand would be the bat that we swung at the paper cup."[2]

The Fluties had a fondness for football as well, and when the family moved to Natick, Massachusetts, in 1975, Doug and Bill joined the high school football team. At first, Bill played quarterback while Doug played safety. Later, the coach switched Bill to wide receiver and Doug to quarterback. Trailing by a point with a minute to go in one game, Doug completed four straight passes to his brother, then kicked the only field goal of his life to win it.

Flutie was like a five-foot eight-inch waterbug, skittering between bigger opponents. Few colleges were interested in him because they thought Flutie was too small to play quarterback. Boston College decided to take a chance. Flutie watched the first three games from the bench. The Eagles were getting blown out by Penn State in the fourth game when Flutie was sent in. He threw a touchdown pass, and the starting job was his. For the next four years he dazzled fans with his heroics. In his Heisman Trophy senior year, he threw 2 late touchdown passes on fourth-down plays to stun mighty Alabama in Birmingham. He set a school record with 6 touchdown passes in a 52–20 romp over North Carolina. Then came the miracle in Miami. An hour after that game, Flutie was still in his uniform, standing in the drizzle, posing for pictures in front of the Orange Bowl scoreboard. It was a storybook ending to a four-year career in which he set the all-time major college passing record, with 10,579 yards. Forty-eight of those yards will be remembered forever.

After his career at Boston College ended, Flutie went on to become one of the best players in the history of the Canadian Football League.

DOUG FLUTIE

BORN: October 23, 1962, Manchester, Maryland.

HIGH SCHOOL: Natick High School, Natick, Massachusetts.

COLLEGE: Boston College.

PRO: Chicago Bears, 1986; New England Patriots, 1987; British
Columbia Lions (CFL), 1990–1991; Calgary Stampeders
(CFL), 1992–1995; Toronto Argonauts (CFL), 1996–1997;
Buffalo Bills, 1998– .

HONORS: Heisman Trophy, 1984; Maxwell Award (outstanding
college player), 1984; O'Brien Quarterback Award, 1984;
Canadian Football League Most Valuable Player,
1991–1994, 1996–1997.

With the ball tucked away, Flutie attempts to run for the first down.

EDDIE GEORGE

Eddie George celebrates after one of his many big runs. At Ohio State, George was a fan favorite.

THE OHIO STATE BUCKEYES WERE UNBEATEN, and they were eyeing the 1996 Rose Bowl. First, they had to beat Illinois, a team they had lost to six times in seven years. Just before kickoff, it was learned that star flanker Terry Glenn would miss the game because of an injury. The Buckeyes knew they had to run the football to win. They turned to Eddie George.

George had been Ohio State's main running threat all season. He had gained 212 yards against Washington, 207 against Notre Dame, and more than 100 in every other game except one, when he got 99. The Ohio Stadium crowds of ninety-five thousand had chanted his name all year. "Ed-die! Ed-die! Ed-die!" they cried. George would shake his head in disbelief. "It's wild," the muscular tailback would say. "It gives me goose bumps."[1]

Against Illinois, George gave the crowd goose bumps. He gained huge chunks of yardage on almost every play, getting 128 yards in the first quarter, 180 by the half, and 64 more on the first play of the third quarter. When he left the game with nearly a quarter to go, he had amassed 314 yards on the ground, scored 2 touchdowns rushing, and caught a pass for a third. Ohio State won easily, 41–3.

Eddie George was raised by his mother in Philadelphia, Pennsylvania. When he was five years old, George kept asking her the same question. "Mom," he would ask, "can I play football?" And Donna George's answer was always the same. "No," she would say. "Not yet, son. Not yet."[2]

When George turned eight, his mother finally said yes, he could play football. In return, George made her a promise. He said that someday he would be a running back for a big college and win the Heisman Trophy. George enrolled in nearby Abington High School with football on his mind. Soon he got caught up with the wrong crowd. By the start of his tenth-grade year, he was failing his classes and getting into trouble. His mother was desperate. She knew her son needed discipline. "She was getting tired of me acting the way I was," George remembers. "Me trying to be Mr. Man. Me thinking that I knew everything."[3] She sent him away to Fork Union Military Academy in Virginia. Soon his grades improved. He grew stronger in the weight room, and faster on the football field. He was maturing from Mr. Man to a man.

Ohio State gave George a full football scholarship. In a game his freshman year, he fumbled twice inside the Illinois 5-yard line and cost his team a victory. After that, and through his sophomore year, he hardly played. But George never sulked on the bench. He simply worked harder to earn back the trust of his coaches. He showed up for practice early and left late. Said Coach John Cooper: "In 33 years as a college coach, I have never been around anybody with a better work ethic, who worked for the team, who did the things he had to do to make himself and his team better than Eddie George."[4]

When George's time came, he was ready. He gained 1,442 yards as a junior. A year later, he destroyed opponents with 1,826 yards and 24 touchdowns. "On a personal level," George said the night he was handed the Heisman Trophy, "this is probably the greatest award I could ever win."[5] His mother smiled as she watched, remembering the promise he had made when he was eight, the promise that he kept.

Now George plays for the Tennessee Oilers of the NFL.

EDDIE GEORGE

BORN: September 24, 1973, Philadelphia, Pennsylvania.

HIGH SCHOOL: Fork Union Military Academy, Fork Union, Virginia.

COLLEGE: Ohio State University.

PRO: Houston Oilers 1996–1997; Tennessee Oilers, 1998– .

HONORS: Heisman Trophy, 1995; Unanimous selection to All-America Team, 1995; Maxwell Award (outstanding college player), 1995; NFL Rookie of the Year, 1996.

Moving to his right, George dodges another would-be tackler.

ARCHIE GRIFFIN

Griffin poses for a picture during halftime of an Ohio State game. Growing up, Griffin dreamed of playing for the Buckeyes.

ARCHIE GRIFFIN

ARCHIE GRIFFIN WAS SITTING ALONE on the bench when he heard Coach Woody Hayes call his name. Hayes was telling Griffin to get in the game. Griffin couldn't believe it. He was a third-stringer, just a freshman. In Ohio State's first game the previous week, he had been in for only one play— and he fumbled that one. But here was the coach, yelling for him to hurry up and get in there.

The Buckeyes trailed North Carolina, 7–0, in their home opener, and their offense couldn't get going. The coach thought maybe Griffin could give his team a lift. With eighty-six thousand fans looking on, Griffin did more than that. He crouched in his tailback spot in the I-formation, took the handoff, and smashed through the line for 6 yards. He carried again for another 6 yards. Then, a couple of plays later, he rammed inside again—another 6 yards.

The Tar Heel defenders grew tired as the game wore on, but Griffin only seemed to get stronger. He battered over tacklers to set up three Ohio State touchdowns. Finally, he ran one in himself from 9 yards out to make the final score 29–14. Moments later it was announced over the loud-speaker that Griffin had broken the school rushing record for a single game—239 yards. Never again would he sit on the bench.

Griffin was born in the shadow of Ohio State's stadium, and he grew up playing football in a nearby lot strewn with rocks and broken glass. He dreamed of someday playing for Ohio State. His father worked two jobs, and sometimes three, to support Archie and his sister and six brothers. Archie delivered newspapers and gave his earnings to his parents to help pay bills. His parents were unable to go to college, but they encouraged their children to work hard and go to college. All seven boys studied hard, played sports, and earned college athletic scholarships.

Griffin was so heavy and slow as a boy that the neighborhood kids called him Tank. His brothers called him Butterball. But Archie was strong. He built muscles by lifting his "barbells," old bottles filled with sand and tied to the ends of a broom handle. He wanted to be a running back, and he was following the advice of a junior high school teacher who told him to always apply the three Ds—desire, determination, and dedication.

Griffin ran everywhere he went, and his speed improved so much that soon he was running sprints for the Eastmoor High School track team. He was so hard to tackle on the football field that his coach, Bob Stuart, called his running "scary."[1]

In four years at Ohio State, Griffin led the Buckeyes to a 40–5–1 record and four Big Ten titles. He started in four straight Rose Bowls, the only player ever to do so. As a junior, he rushed for a school-record 1,695 yards to win the Heisman Trophy. He made football history the following year by winning the Heisman again. Griffin remains the only player to have won the Heisman twice.

Griffin's biggest gains were always made with children in mind. As a college junior, he ran for A Better Chance—for every yard he gained, people in the community donated money to help disadvantaged children. He also graduated early to free up time in the spring to visit elementary schools. "I learned a lot about football while I was at Ohio State," Griffin said, "but I also learned a lot about being a person."[2]

Griffin went on to play seven seasons with the Cincinnati Bengals.

ARCHIE GRIFFIN

BORN: August 21, 1954, Columbus, Ohio.

HIGH SCHOOL: Eastmoor High School, Columbus, Ohio.

COLLEGE: Ohio State University.

PRO: Cincinnati Bengals, 1976–1982.

HONORS: Heisman Trophy, 1974–1975; Maxwell Award (outstanding college player), 1975; College Football Hall of Fame.

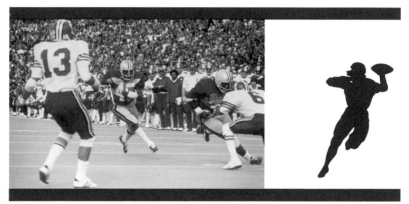

Archie Griffin looks for running room against the Indiana Hoosiers. Griffin is the only player to have won the Heisman Trophy twice.

PAUL HORNUNG

PAUL HORNUNG STOOD ALONE under the goalpost, waiting for the Iowa team to kick off. A crowd of sixty thousand, the biggest ever to watch a Notre Dame game at South Bend, Indiana up to that time, had just seen the Hawkeyes take a 14–7 lead. There were fewer than ten minutes left. Hornung was The Golden Boy, a handsome blond who played quarterback, halfback, fullback, kick returner, safety, and kicker for Notre Dame. He could do everything. But could he save his team from defeat?

Hornung returned the kickoff up the middle 23 yards to the Notre Dame 37. Then, playing quarterback, he passed for 17, 14, and 15 yards to get the Fighting Irish to the Iowa 17. Fewer than six minutes remained. Hornung dropped back to pass again, broke free of a tackler, retreated to his 40, and arched a perfect pass to receiver Jim Morse for a touchdown. Then he kicked the extra point to tie the game.

Hornung was not through. He kicked off, raced down-field and, unassisted, tackled the Iowa runner on the 2-yard line. Then he led a defensive stand that forced Iowa to punt. Notre Dame got the ball back on the Iowa 43. On third down, Hornung scrambled with the ball to the 30, but a penalty wiped out the play. Hornung kept cool. He threw a strike downfield to Morse, to put the Irish in scoring range. With time running out, Hornung kicked a 28-yard field goal to win the game. The Irish won 8 times in 1955, thanks mostly to Hornung, who finished fifth in the Heisman Trophy voting, behind winner Hopalong Cassady.

In 1956, Hornung's senior year, Notre Dame won only two of its ten games. Hornung was so valiant in defeat,

Paul Hornung was a great all-around athlete. While at Notre Dame, he played six different positions.

PAUL HORNUNG

though, it was impossible for Heisman voters to ignore him. He led his team in rushing, passing, scoring, kickoff returns, punt returns, punting, and passes broken up, and was second in tackles and interceptions. He edged Johnny Majors of unbeaten Tennessee, 1,066 points to 994, to win the award. He remains the only Heisman winner to play for a losing team.

Paul Hornung was born two days before Christmas in 1935, and his father left home shortly thereafter. He was raised by his strict mother and an uncle who predicted that Hornung would become an All-American star for Notre Dame. Hornung was taller than most boys his age, and he played quarterback as early as sixth grade at St. Patrick's Grammar School. At Flaget High School, he was voted the top football player in Kentucky, and even the state's governor came to watch him play. He got mostly As in school, and ranked among the top ten in his class.

After his brilliant college career, Hornung joined the NFL's Green Bay Packers. With Hornung darting through defenses at halfback, the Packers became a dynasty. Hornung led the league in scoring three straight years, from 1959 to 1961. Coach Vince Lombardi called him "the most versatile man who ever played the game."[1]

PAUL HORNUNG

BORN: December 23, 1935, Louisville, Kentucky.

HIGH SCHOOL: Flaget High School, Louisville, Kentucky.

COLLEGE: University of Notre Dame.

PRO: Green Bay Packers, 1957–1962, 1964–1966.

HONORS: Heisman Trophy, 1956; College Football Hall of Fame; NFL Most Valuable Player, 1961; Pro Football Hall of Fame, 1986.

Hornung is now a member of the College Football Hall of Fame and the Pro Football Hall of Fame.

BARRY SANDERS

Barry Sanders breaks through the Nebraska defensive line.

BARRY SANDERS

SURE, THE TEXAS A&M AGGIES THOUGHT, Barry Sanders had run for 178 yards and 4 scores in the season opener to stomp Miami-Ohio, 52–20. But there was no way he could dodge and dart his way through the mighty A&M defense. As the game with Oklahoma State came to a close, however, the faces of the A&M players told the story. They were tired. Somber. They could do nothing to stop Sanders, who wiggled his way for 157 yards and two touchdowns, to lead Oklahoma State to a 52–15 victory.

Sanders started the 1988 season as the replacement for Thurman Thomas. He finished it as the most prolific running back in college history. A 100-yard game is the benchmark for a running back. Barry Sanders shattered that mark. He averaged more than 200 a game. He had the first 300-yard game in school history. He followed that with a second 300-yard game, then a third, then a fourth. There wasn't a defense in the land that could stop him.

Sanders grew up in Wichita, Kansas, living with his parents, two brothers, and eight sisters. His brother Byron, older by a year, was Barry's guide. Everything Byron did, Barry copied. So when Byron decided to join his junior high school football team, Barry did too. Barry was barely 5-feet tall and weighed just 103 pounds. He was the smallest player on the team, but he was also the fastest. The coach put him at cornerback.

Barry Sanders didn't become a running back until his senior year of high school. In his first game for Wichita North, he was given the ball on five plays. He scored touchdowns on 4 of them. He went on to set the school's single-season rushing record. But it didn't matter that Sanders could scoot through defenses. He was barely 5-feet 6-inches tall, and most colleges considered him too small for Division I football.

Oklahoma State coach Pat Jones took a chance. He gave Sanders a full scholarship and let him return kicks. When Thurman Thomas needed a rest, the coach sent Sanders in as the replacement. Sanders gained 138 yards in one game against a lowly opponent, but he didn't do much else. His sophomore year was better, with three 100-yard games, but he still stood in Thomas's shadow. He concentrated on his classes, hoping to get a business degree in four years. His chance came his junior year, and he ran with it. He rushed for more yards than anyone ever had rushed in a season— 2,628. He scored more touchdowns—39. He broke 34 NCAA records in all. Being awarded the Heisman Trophy was just a formality. There was no second choice.

Sanders was such a gifted runner that he left school a year early to join the pros. That business degree would have to wait. Instead of breaking more college records as a senior, Sanders ran wild in the NFL as the Rookie of the Year for the Detroit Lions. In fact, he has a chance to break Walter Payton's career rushing record. More than ten years later, pro defenses are asking the same question Texas A&M did in 1988: "How do we stop this guy?"

BARRY SANDERS

BORN: July 16, 1968, Wichita, Kansas.

HIGH SCHOOL: Wichita North High School, Wichita, Kansas.

COLLEGE: Oklahoma State University.

PRO: Detroit Lions 1989– .

HONORS: Heisman Trophy, 1988; Maxwell Award (outstanding college player), 1988; NFL Most Valuable Player, 1991, 1997.

In 1988, Barry Sanders set an NCAA record for the most yards rushing in a season, with 2,628.

ROGER STAUBACH

ROGER STAUBACH WAS PLAYING IN DALLAS, where years later he would be a star for the NFL's Cowboys. But this was 1963, and Staubach was a junior quarterback for the United States Naval Academy. The Midshipmen hadn't lost all year, but they were caught in a whirlwind battle with the high-powered Southern Methodist Mustangs.

Staubach's ability to escape would-be tacklers had earned him the nickname Roger the Dodger. But the SMU defenders were roughing him up, twice sending him to the sideline with an injured shoulder. Staubach returned each time to lead his offense to touchdowns, and the Middies were out in front, 25–13, in the third quarter. But SMU scored twice to take the lead, 26–25. Navy took possession to start the fourth quarter, and Staubach ran 11 yards on the first play, but he was hit hard and knocked unconscious. Revived with smelling salts by the team trainer, Staubach drove his team to a field goal and the lead. But SMU scored a touchdown to move in front, 32–28.

With barely two minutes left, Staubach tried once more to lead his team. He raced around end for 16 yards. He passed for 14 more. He bolted up the middle for 15 more. Time was running out. He passed for 12 more. The Middies had reached the 3-yard line. Two seconds remained. There was time for one more play. Staubach threw to the end zone. The ball bounced off his receiver's hands. Navy lost, and Staubach left the field in tears. It was his team's only loss of the year. But even in defeat, Staubach proved he was a winner.

Roger Staubach grew up in Cincinnati, Ohio, where he

While he was at the U.S. Naval Academy, Roger Staubach was known as "Roger the Dodger" because of his ability to elude the defense.

ROGER STAUBACH

began playing football at an early age. His seventh-grade St. John's Eagles team didn't win one game, but with Staubach playing halfback and flanker, his eighth-grade team went undefeated. In a 21–20 victory over rival Assumption Junior High, Staubach ran back the opening kickoff for a touchdown, caught a 50-yard pass for another, and ran for a third. He went on to become All-Ohio in football, basketball, and baseball at Purcell High School.

Staubach was a patriotic, religious person who accepted an appointment to the Naval Academy. But he flunked his English entrance exam, and had to spend a year at the New Mexico Military Institute. He studied hard at English and passed the exam the following year. "It's funny," Staubach said when he arrived in Annapolis, Maryland, "but English is now one of my best subjects."[1]

Staubach watched the first three games from the sideline his sophomore year, before Coach Wayne Hardin finally sent him in against Cornell. Staubach never left the lineup. He threw for a touchdown and ran for 2 more against Cornell, threw 2 touchdowns to beat Boston College. He then completed all 8 of his passes for 192 yards to beat Pittsburgh. When he completed 11 of 13 passes and ran for 2 touchdowns to lead Navy to a stunning 34–14 upset over rival Army, Coach Hardin gushed afterward, "He's tremendous, sensational, fantastic! He's the best running, throwing, anything. He should be the greatest quarterback in Naval Academy history."[2]

Staubach won the Heisman Trophy his junior year, but suffered through injuries in his senior season. Upon graduation, he remained with the Academy for four years, fulfilling his duties as a naval officer. In 1969, he was a twenty-seven-year-old NFL rookie. Two years later, he became a starter for the Cowboys, and he guided them to two Super Bowl titles.

ROGER STAUBACH

BORN: February 5, 1942, Cincinnati, Ohio.

HIGH SCHOOL: Purcell High School, Cincinnati, Ohio.

COLLEGE: United States Naval Academy.

PRO: Dallas Cowboys, 1969–1979.

HONORS: Heisman Trophy, 1963; Maxwell Award (outstanding college player), 1963; College Football Hall of Fame; NFL Most Valuable Player, 1971; Super Bowl VI MVP; Pro Football Hall of Fame, 1985.

Because of his obligation to serve in the U.S. Navy, Staubach had to wait until four years after his last college season to play in the NFL.

CHAPTER NOTES

Marcus Allen

1. Douglas S. Looney, "2,000," *Sports Illustrated*, November 23, 1981, p. 40.

2. Ibid.

3. *USC Trojans Media Guide*, 1982.

4. Ibid.

5. Bob Oates, "The Right Man for the Wrong Reason," *Los Angeles Times*, October 22, 1981, p. 7.

6. John T. Brady, *The Heisman—A Symbol of Excellence* (New York: Atheneum, 1984), p. 204.

7. Oates, p. 1.

Tim Brown

1. *Notre Dame Football Guide*, 1987, p. 36.

2. Ibid.

3. Ibid., p. 37.

4. Ibid., p. 35.

Ernie Davis

1. Bill Libby, *Heroes of the Heisman Trophy* (New York: Hawthorn Books, 1973), p. 135.

2. Sandy Grady, "Davis Had Full Life at 23," *The Philadelphia Sunday Bulletin*, May 19, 1963, p. 1.

3. John T. Brady, *The Heisman—A Symbol of Excellence* (New York: Atheneum, 1984), p. 134.

4. Arthur Daley, "The Happy Warrior," *The New York Times*, May 21, 1963, p. 36.

Tony Dorsett

1. *Pittsburgh Panthers Media Guide*, 1995, p. 132.

2. John Devaney, *Winners of the Heisman Trophy* (New York: Walker and Company, 1990), p. 89.

3. Gene Duffey, "Dorsett: The Turtle Turned Hare," *Rochester Times-Union*, December 23, 1975, p. 1.

4. John T. Brady, *The Heisman—A Symbol of Excellence* (New York: Atheneum, 1984), p. 180.

5. Duffey, p. 1.

Doug Flutie

1. Leigh Montville, "BC, Flutie Get Storybook Victory," *Boston Globe*, November 23, 1984, p. 33.

2. John Devaney, *Winners of the Heisman Trophy* (New York: Walker and Company, 1990), p. 10.

Eddie George

1. Tim May, "Buckeye Fans Spur George in Heisman Race," *Columbus* [Ohio] *Dispatch*, November 17, 1995, p. 1.

2. Tim May, "George Wins the Heisman," *Columbus Dispatch*, December 10, 1995, p. 1.

3. John Roe, "Mother Knows Best for Buckeye's George," *Minneapolis Star Tribune*, November 4, 1995, p. 1.

4. May, "George Wins the Heisman," p. 1.

5. Tim May, "George's Journey Ends in Triumph," *Columbus Dispatch*, December 11, 1995, p. 1.

Archie Griffin

1. Edward F. Dolan, *Archie Griffin* (Garden City, N.Y.: Doubleday & Company, 1977), p. 26.

2. *Ohio State Media Guide*, 1996, p. 212.

Paul Hornung

1. John T. Brady, *The Heisman—A Symbol of Excellence* (New York: Atheneum, 1984), p. 110.

Roger Staubach

1. Alan Goldstein, "Staubach of Navy," *The Baltimore Sun*, November 3, 1963, p. 13.

2. Ibid.

INDEX

A
Allen, Marcus, 6–9

B
Berwanger, Jay, 4–5
Bicknell, Jack, 22
Billick, Dean, 20
Brown, Jim, 16
Brown, Tim, 10–13

C
Carney, John, 11
Cassady, Hopalong, 34
Cooper, John, 28

D
Davis, Ernie, 14–17
Dorsett, Tony, 18–21

F
Faust, Gerry, 6
Flutie, Bill, 24
Flutie, Doug, 22–25

G
Garrett, Mike, 8
George, Eddie, 26–29
Glenn, Terry, 27
Griffin, Archie, 30–33

H
Hardin, Wayne, 44
Hayes, Woody, 31
Heisman, John W., 4

Holtz, Lou, 12
Hornung, Paul, 34–37

J
Jackson, John, 6
Jones, Harry, 20
Jones, Pat, 40

K
Kennedy, John F., 16

L
Lombardi, Vince, 36

M
Majors, Johnny, 18, 36
Mitchell, Bobby, 16
Modell, Art, 16
Morse, Jim, 34

P
Paterno, Joe, 18
Payton, Walter, 40
Phelan, Gerard, 22

S
Sanders, Barry, 38–41
Sanders, Byron, 39
Schwartzwalder, Ben, 15
Staubach, Roger, 42–45
Stuart, Bob, 32

T
Thomas, Thurman, 39, 40
Tollner, Ted, 11